CW01649348

Dad,

Happy Xmas 2006

Love from Michael

THE DUNCIAD

Alexander Pope

Table of Contents

THE DUNCIAD

Alexander Pope

TO Dr. JONATHAN SWIFT

Book the First.

ARGUMENT TO Book the First.

THE Proposition, the Invocation, and the Inscription. Then the Original of the great Empire of Dulness, and cause of the continuance thereof. The College of the Goddess in the City, with her private Academy for Poets in particular; the Governors of it, and the four Cardinal Virtues. Then the Poem hastes into the midst of things, presenting her, on the evening of a Lord Mayor's day, revolving the long succession of her Sons, and the glories past and to come. She fixes her eye on Bays to be the Instrument of that great Event which is the Subject of the Poem. He is described pensive among his Books, giving up the Cause, and apprehending the Period of her Empire: After debating whether to betake himself to the Church, or to Gaming, or to Party–writing, he raises an Altar of proper books, and (making first his solemn prayer and declaration) purposes thereon to sacrifice all his unsuccessful writings. As the pile is kindled, the Goddess beholding the flame from her seat, flies and puts it out by casting upon it the poem of Thulé. She forthwith reveals herself to him, transports him to her Temple, unfolds her Arts, and initiates him into her Mysteries; then announcing the death of Eusden the Poet Laureate, anoints him, carries him to Court, and proclaims him Successor.

The Mighty Mother, and her Son who brings
The Smithfield Muses to the ear of Kings,

I sing. Say you, her instruments the Great!
Call'd to this work by Dulness, Jove, and Fate;

You by whose care, in vain decry'd and curst,
Still Dunce the second reigns like Dunce the first;

Say how the Goddess bade Britannia sleep,
And pour'd her Spirit o'er the land and deep.
In eldest time, e'er mortals writ or read,
E'er Pallas issu'd from the Thund'rer's head,
Dulness o'er all possess'd her ancient right,
Daughter of Chaos and eternal Night:
Fate in their dotage this fair Ideot gave,
Gross as her sire, and as her mother grave,

Laborious, heavy, busy, bold, and blind,
She rul'd, in native Anarchy, the mind.
Still her old Empire to restore she tries,
For, born a Goddess, Dulness never dies.
O Thou! whatever title please thine ear,
Dean, Drapier, Bickerstaff, or Gulliver!
Whether thou chuse Cervantes' serious air,
Or laugh and shake in Rab'lais' easy chair,
Or praise the Court, or magnify Mankind,
Or thy griev'd Country's copper chains unbind;
From thy Boeotia tho' her Pow'r retires,
Mourn not, my Swift, at ought our Realm acquires,
Here pleas'd behold her mighty wings out–spread
To hatch a new Saturnian age of Lead.
Close to those walls where Folly holds her throne,
And laughs to think Monroe would take her down,

Where o'er the gates, by his fam'd father's hand
Great Cibber's brazen, brainless brothers stand;
One Cell there is, conceal'd from vulgar eye,
The Cave of Poverty and Poetry.
Keen, hollow winds howl thro' the bleak recess,
Emblem of Music caus'd by Emptiness.
Hence Bards, like Proteus long in vain ty'd down,
Escape in Monsters, and amaze the town.

Hence Miscellanies spring, the weekly boast
Of Curl's chaste press, and Lintot's rubric post:
Hence hymning Tyburn's elegiac lines,
Hence Journals, Medleys, Merc'ries, Magazines:
Sepulchral Lyes, our holy walls to grace,
And New–year Odes, and all the Grub–street race.
In clouded Majesty here Dulness shone;
Four guardian Virtues, round, support her throne:
Fierce champion Fortitude, that knows no fears
Of hisses, blows, or want, or loss of ears:

Calm Temperance, whose blessings those partake
Who hunger, and who thirst for scribling sake:
Prudence, whose glass presents th'approaching jayl:
Poetic Justice, with her lifted scale,
Where, in nice balance, truth with gold she weighs,
And solid pudding against empty praise.
Here she beholds the Chaos dark and deep,
Where nameless Somethings in their causes sleep,
'Till genial Jacob, or a warm Third day,
Call forth each mass, a Poem, or a Play:

How hints, like spawn, scarce quick in embryo lie,
How new–born nonsense first is taught to cry,
Maggots half–form'd in rhyme exactly meet,
And learn to crawl upon poetic feet.
Here one poor word an hundred clenches makes,
And ductile dulness new meanders takes;
There motley Images her fancy strike,
Figures ill pair'd, and Similies unlike.
She sees a Mob of Metaphors advance,
Pleas'd with the madness of the mazy dance:
How Tragedy and Comedy embrace;
How Farce and Epic get a jumbled race;

How Time himself stands still at her command,
Realms shift their place, and Ocean turns to land.
Here gay Description Ægypt glads with show'rs,
Or gives to Zembla fruits, to Barca flow'rs;
Glitt'ring with ice here hoary hills are seen,
There painted vallies of eternal green,
In cold December fragrant chaplets blow,
And heavy harvests nod beneath the snow.
All these, and more, the cloud–compelling Queen
Beholds thro' fogs, that magnify the scene.
She, tinsel'd o'er in robes of varying hues,

With self–applause her wild creation views;
Sees momentary monsters rise and fall,
And with her own fools–colours gilds them all.
'Twas on the day, when — rich and grave,
Like Cimon, triumph'd both on land and wave:

(Pomps without guilt, of bloodless swords and maces,
Glad chains, warm furs, broad banners, and broad faces)
Now Night descending, the proud scene was o'er,
But liv'd, in Settle's numbers, one day more.
Now May'rs and Shrieves all hush'd and satiate lay,
Yet eat, in dreams, the custard of the day;
While pensive Poets painful vigils keep,
Sleepless themselves, to give their readers sleep.
Much to the mindful Queen the feast recalls
What City Swans once sung within the walls;

Much she revolves their arts, their ancient praise,
And sure succession down from Heywood's days.
She saw, with joy, the line immortal run,
Each sire imprest and glaring in his son:
So watchful Bruin forms, with plastic care,
Each growing lump, and brings it to a Bear.
She saw old Pryn in restless Daniel shine,
And Eusden eke out Blackmore's endless line;

She saw slow Philips creep like Tate's poor page,
And all the mighty Mad in Dennis rage.
In each she marks her Image full exprest,
But chief in Bays's monster–breeding breast;

Bays, form'd by nature Stage and Town to bless,
And act, and be, a Coxcomb with success.

Dulness with transport eyes the lively Dunce,
Remembring she herself was Pertness once.

THE DUNCIAD

Now (shame to Fortune!) an ill Run at Play
Blank'd his bold visage, and a thin Third day:
Swearing and supperless the Hero sate,
Blasphem'd his Gods, the Dice, and damn'd his Fate.
Then gnaw'd his pen, then dash'd it on the ground,
Sinking from thought to thought, a vast profound!
Plung'd for his sense, but found no bottom there,
Yet wrote and flounder'd on, in mere despair.
Round him much Embryo, much Abortion lay,
Much future Ode, and abdicated Play;

Nonsense precipitate, like running Lead,
That slip'd thro' Cracks and Zig–zags of the Head;
All that on Folly Frenzy could beget,
Fruits of dull Heat, and Sooterkins of Wit.
Next, o'er his Books his eyes began to roll,
In pleasing memory of all he stole,
How here he sipp'd, how there he plunder'd snug
And suck'd all o'er, like an industrious Bug.
Here lay poor Fletcher's half–eat scenes, and here
The Frippery of crucify'd Moliere;
There hapless Shakespear, yet of Tibbald sore,
Wish'd he had blotted for himself before.

The rest on Out–side merit but presume,
Or serve (like other Fools) to fill a room;
Such with their shelves as due proportion hold,
Or their fond Parents drest in red and gold;
Or where the pictures for the page attone,
And Quarles is sav'd by Beauties not his own.
Here swells the shelf with Ogilby the great;
There, stamp'd with arms, Newcastle shines complete:
Here all his suff'ring brotherhood retire,
And 'scape the martyrdom of jakes and fire:
A Gothic Library! of Greece and Rome
Well purg'd, and worthy Settle, Banks, and Broome.

But, high above, more solid Learning shone,
The Classics of an Age that heard of none;
There Caxton slept, with Wynkyn at his side,
One clasp'd in wood, and one in strong cow–hide;
There, sav'd by spice, like Mummies, many a year,
Dry Bodies of Divinity appear:

De Lyra there a dreadful front extends,
And here the groaning shelves Philemon bends.
Of these twelve volumes, twelve of amplest size,
Redeem'd from tapers and defrauded pies,
Inspir'd he seizes: These an altar raise:
An hecatomb of pure, unsully'd lays
That altar crowns: A folio Common–place
Founds the whole pile, of all his works the base:
Quartos, octavos, shape the less'ning pyre;
A twisted Birth–day Ode completes the spire.
Then he: Great Tamer of all human art!
First in my care, and ever at my heart;
Dulness! whose good old cause I yet defend,
With whom my Muse began, with whom shall end;
E'er since Sir Fopling's Periwig was Praise,
To the last honours of the Butt and Bays:

O thou! of Bus'ness the directing soul!
To this our head like byass to the bowl,
Which, as more pond'rous, made its aim more true,
Obliquely wadling to the mark in view:
O! ever gracious to perplex'd mankind,
Still spread a healing mist before the mind;
And lest we err by Wit's wild dancing light,
Secure us kindly in our native night.
Or, if to Wit a coxcomb make pretence,
Guard the sure barrier between that and Sense;
Or quite unravel all the reas'ning thread,
And hang some curious cobweb in its stead!

As, forc'd from wind–guns, lead itself can fly,
And pond'rous slugs cut swiftly thro the sky;

As clocks to weight their nimble motion owe,
The wheels above urg'd by the load below:
Me Emptiness, and Dulness could inspire,
And were my Elasticity, and Fire.
Some Dæmon stole my pen (forgive th'offence)
And once betray'd me into common sense:
Else all my Prose and Verse were much the same;
This, prose on stilts; that, poetry fall'n lame.
Did on the stage my Fops appear confin'd?
My Life gave ampler lessons to mankind.
Did the dead Letter unsuccessful prove?
The brisk Example never fail'd to move.
Yet sure had Heav'n decreed to save the State,
Heav'n had decreed these works a longer date.
Could Troy be sav'd by any single hand,
This grey–goose weapon must have made her stand.
What can I now? my Fletcher cast aside,
Take up the Bible, once my better guide?

Or tread the path by vent'rous Heroes trod,
This Box my Thunder, this right hand my God?
Or chair'd at White's amidst the Doctors sit,
Teach Oaths to Gamesters, and to Nobles Wit?
Or bidst thou rather Party to embrace?
(A friend to Party thou, and all her race;
'Tis the same rope at different ends they twist;
To Dulness Ridpath is as dear as Mist.)

Shall I, like Curtius, desp'rate in my zeal,
O'er head and ears plunge for the Commonweal?
Or rob Rome's ancient geese of all their glories,
And cackling save the Monarchy of Tories?
Hold—to the Minister I more incline;

To serve his cause, O Queen! is serving thine.

And see! thy very Gazetteers give o'er,
Ev'n Ralph repents, and Henly writes no more.
What then remains? Ourself. Still, still remain
Cibberian forehead, and Cibberian brain.
This brazen Brightness, to the 'Squire so dear;
This polish'd Hardness, that reflects the Peer;
This arch Absurd, that wit and fool delights;
This Mess, toss'd up of Hockley–hole and White's;
Where Dukes and Butchers join to wreathe my crown,
At once the Bear and Fiddle of the town.
O born in sin, and forth in folly brought!
Works damn'd, or to be damn'd! (your father's fault)
Go, purify'd by flames ascend the sky,
My better and more christian progeny!

Unstain'd, untouch'd, and yet in maiden sheets;
While all your smutty sisters walk the streets.
Ye shall not beg, like gratis–given Bland,
Sent with a Pass, and vagrant thro' the land;
Not sail, with Ward, to Ape–and–monkey climes,
Where vile Mundungus trucks for viler rhymes;
Not sulphur–tipt, emblaze an Ale–house fire;
Not wrap up Oranges, to pelt your sire!
O! pass more innocent, in infant state,
To the mild Limbo of our Father Tate:

Or peaceably forgot, at once be blest
In Shadwell's bosom with eternal Rest!
Soon to that mass of Nonsense to return,
Where things destroy'd are swept to things unborn.
With that, a Tear (portentous sign of Grace!)
Stole from the Master of the sev'nfold Face:
And thrice he lifted high the Birth–day brand,
And thrice he dropt it from his quiv'ring hand;

Then lights the structure, with averted eyes:
The rowling smokes involve the sacrifice.
The op'ning clouds disclose each work by turns,
Now flames the Cid, and now Perolla burns;

Great Cæsar roars, and hisses in the fires;
King John in silence modestly expires:
No merit now the dear Nonjuror claims,
Moliere's old stubble in a moment flames.
Tears gush'd again, as from pale Priam's eyes
When the last blaze sent Ilion to the skies.
Rowz'd by the light, old Dulness heav'd the head;
Then snatch'd a sheet of Thulè from her bed,
Sudden she flies, and whelms it o'er the pyre;
Down sink the flames, and with a hiss expire.
Her ample presence fills up all the place;
A veil of fogs dilates her awful face:
Great in her charms! as when on Shrieves and May'rs
She looks, and breathes herself into their airs.
She bids him wait her to her sacred Dome:
Well pleas'd he enter'd, and confess'd his home.
So Spirits ending their terrestrial race,
Ascend, and recognize their Native Place.

This the Great Mother dearer held than all
The clubs of Quidnuncs, or her own Guild–hall:
Here stood her Opium, her she nurs'd her Owls,
And here she plann'd th'Imperial seat of Fools.
Here to her Chosen all her works she shews;
Prose swell'd to verse, verse loit'ring into prose:
How random thoughts now meaning chance to find,
Now leave all memory of sense behind:
How Prologues into Prefaces decay,
And these to Notes are fritter'd quite away:
How Index–learning turns no student pale,
Yet holds the eel of science by the tail:

THE DUNCIAD

How, with less reading than makes felons scape,
Less human genius than God gives an ape,
Small thanks to France, and none to Rome or Greece,
A past, vamp'd, future, old, reviv'd, new piece,

'Twixt Plautus, Fletcher, Shakespear, and Corneille,
Can make a Cibber, Tibbald, or Ozell.
The Goddess then, o'er his anointed head,
With mystic words, the sacred Opium shed.
And lo! her bird, (a monster of a fowl,
Something betwixt a Heideggre and owl,)

Perch'd on his crown. "All hail! and hail again,
My son! the promis'd land expects thy reign.
Know, Eusden thirsts no more for sack or praise;
He sleeps among the dull of ancient days;
Safe, where no Critics damn, no duns molest,
Where wretched Withers, Ward, and Gildon rest,
And high–born Howard, more majestic sire,
With Fool of Quality compleats the quire.
Thou Cibber! thou, his Laurel shalt support,
Folly, my son, has still a Friend at Court.
Lift up your Gates, ye Princes, see him come!
Sound, sound ye Viols, be the Cat–call dumb!
Bring, bring the madding Bay, the drunken Vine;
The creeping, dirty, courtly Ivy join.
And thou! his Aid de camp, lead on my sons,
Light–arm'd with Points, Antitheses, and Puns.

Let Bawdry, Bilingsgate, my daughters dear,
Support his front, and Oaths bring up the rear:
And under his, and under Archer's wing,
Gaming and Grub–street skulk behind the King.
O! when shall rise a Monarch all our own,
And I, a Nursing–mother, rock the throne,
'Twixt Prince and People close the Curtain draw,

Shade him from Light, and cover him from Law;
Fatten the Courtier, starve the learned band,
And suckle Armies, and dry–nurse the land:

'Till Senates nod to Lullabies divine,
And all be sleep, as at an Ode of thine.
She ceas'd. Then swells the Chapel–royal throat:
God save king Cibber! mounts in ev'ry note.
Familiar White's, God save king Colley! cries;
God save king Colley! Drury–lane replies:
To Needham's quick the voice triumphal rode,
But pious Needham dropt the name of God;
Back to the Devil the last echoes roll,
And Coll! each Butcher roars at Hockley–hole.
So when Jove's block descended from on high
(As sings thy great forefather Ogilby)

Loud thunder to its bottom shook the bog,
And the hoarse nation croak'd, God save King Log! The End of the First Book.

Book the Second.

ARGUMENT.

The King being proclaimed, the solemnity is graced with public Games and sports of various kinds; not instituted by the Hero, as by Æneas in Virgil, but for greater honour by the Goddess in person (in like manner as the games Pythia, Isthmia, &c. were anciently said to be ordained by the Gods, and as Thetis herself appearing, according to Homer, Odyss. 24. proposed the prizes in honour of her son Achilles.) Hither flock the Poets and Critics, attended, as is but just, with their Patrons and Booksellers. The Goddess is first pleased, for her disport, to propose games to the Booksellers, and setteth up the Phantom of a Poet, which they contend to overtake. The Races described, with their divers accidents. Next, the game for a Poetess. Then follow the Exercises for the Poets, of tickling, vociferating, diving: The first holds forth the arts and practices of Dedicators, the second of Disputants and fustian Poets, the third of profound, dark, and dirty Party–writers. Lastly, for the Critics, the Goddess proposes (with great propriety) an Exercise, not of their parts, but their patience, in hearing the works of two voluminous Authors, one in verse, and the other in prose, deliberately read, without sleeping: The various effects of which, with the several degrees and manners of their operation, are here set forth; 'till the whole number, not of Critics only, but of spectators, actors, and all present, fall fast asleep; which naturally and necessarily ends the games.

High on a gorgeous seat, that far out–shone
Henley's gilt tub, or Fleckno's Irish throne,

Or that where on her Curls the Public pours,
All–bounteous, fragrant Grains and Golden show'rs,
Great Cibber sate: The proud Parnassian sneer,
The conscious simper, and the jealous leer,
Mix on his look: All eyes direct their rays
On him, and crowds turn Coxcombs as they gaze.
His Peers shine round him with reflected grace,
New edge their dulness, and new bronze their face.
So from the Sun's broad beam, in shallow urns
Heav'ns twinkling Sparks draw light, and point their horns.
Not with more glee, by hands Pontific crown'd,
With scarlet hats wide–waving circled round,
Rome in her Capitol saw Querno sit,
Thron'd on sev'n hills, the Antichrist of wit.
And now the Queen, to glad her sons, proclaims
By herald Hawkers, high heroic Games.
They summon all her Race: An endless band
Pours forth, and leaves unpeopled half the land.
A motley mixture! in long wigs, in bags,
In silks, in crapes, in Garters, and in rags,
From drawing rooms, from colleges, from garrets,
On horse, on foot, in hacks, and gilded chariots:

All who true Dunces in her cause appear'd,
And all who knew those Dunces to reward.
Amid that area wide they took their stand,
Where the tall may–pole once o'er–look'd the Strand;
But now (so Anne and Piety ordain)
A Church collects the saints of Drury–lane.
With Authors, Stationers obey'd the call,
(The field of glory is a field for all.)
Glory, and gain, th'industrious tribe provoke;
And gentle Dulness ever loves a joke.
A Poet's form she plac'd before their eyes,
And bade the nimblest racer seize the prize;

No meagre, muse–rid mope, adust and thin,
In a dun night–gown of his own loose skin;
But such a bulk as no twelve bards could raise,
Twelve starv'ling bards of these degen'rate days.
All as a partridge plump, full–fed, and fair,
She form'd this image of well–body'd air;
With pert flat eyes she window'd well its head;
A brain of feathers, and a heart of lead;
And empty words she gave, and sounding strain,
But senseless, lifeless! idol void and vain!
Never was dash'd out, at one lucky hit,
A fool, so just a copy of a wit;

So like, that critics said, and courtiers swore,
A Wit it was, and call'd the phantom More.
All gaze with ardour: Some a poet's name,
Others a sword–knot and lac'd suit inflame.
But lofty Lintot in the circle rose:
"This prize is mine; who tempt it are my foes;

With me began this genius, and shall end."
He spoke: and who with Lintot shall contend? Fear held them mute. Alone, untaught to fear,

Stood dauntless Curl; "Behold that rival here!

"The race by vigour, not by vaunts is won;
"So take the hindmost, Hell."—He said, and run.
Swift as a bard the bailiff leaves behind,
He left huge Lintot, and out–strip'd the wind.
As when a dab–chick waddles thro' the copse
On feet and wings, and flies, and wades, and hops;
So lab'ring on, with shoulders, hands, and head,
Wide as a wind–mill all his figures spread,

With arms expanded Bernard rows his state,
And left–legg'd Jacob seems to emulate.
Full in the middle way there stood a lake,
Which Curl's Corinna chanc'd that morn to make:
(Such was her wont, at early dawn to drop
Her evening cates before his neighbour's shop,)
Here fortun'd Curl to slide; loud shout the band,
And Bernard! Bernard! rings thro' all the Strand.
Obscene with filth the miscreant lies bewray'd,
Fal'n in the plash his wickedness had laid:

Then first (if Poets aught of truth declare)
The caitiff Vaticide conceiv'd a pray'r.
Hear Jove! whose name my bards and I adore,
As much at least as any God's, or more;
And him and his, if more devotion warms,
Down with the Bible, up with the Pope's Arms.
A place there is, betwixt earth, air, and seas,
Where, from Ambrosia, Jove retires for ease.
There in his seat two spacious vents appear,
On this he sits, to that he leans his ear,

And hears the various vows of fond mankind;
Some beg an eastern, some a western wind:
All vain petitions, mounting to the sky,

With reams abundant this abode supply;
Amus'd he reads, and then returns the bills
Sign'd with that Ichor which from Gods distils.
In office here fair Cloacina stands,
And ministers to Jove with purest hands.
Forth from the heap she pick'd her Vot'ry's pray'r,
And plac'd it next him, a distinction rare!
Oft had the Goddess heard her servant's call,
From her black grottos near the Temple–wall,
List'ning delighted to the jest unclean
Of link–boys vile, and watermen obscene;
Where as he fish'd her nether realms for Wit,
She oft had favour'd him, and favours yet.
Renew'd by ordure's sympathetic force,
As oil'd with magic juices for the course,

Vig'rous he rises; from th'effluvia strong
Imbibes new life, and scours and stinks along;
Re–passes Lintot, vindicates the race,
Nor heeds the brown dishonours of his face.
And now the victor stretch'd his eager hand
Where the tall Nothing stood, or seem'd to stand;
A shapeless shade, it melted from his sight,
Like forms in clouds, or visions of the night.
To seize his papers, Curl, was next thy care;
His papers light, fly diverse, tost in air;
Songs, sonnets, epigrams the winds uplift,
And whisk 'em back to Evans, Young, and Swift.

Th'embroider'd suit at least he deem'd his prey;
That suit an unpay'd taylor snatch'd away.
No rag, no scrap, of all the beau, or wit,
That once so flutter'd, and that once so writ.
Heav'n rings with laughter: Of the laughter vain,
Dulness, good Queen, repeats the jest again.
Three wicked imps, of her own Grubstreet choir,

She deck'd like Congreve, Addison, and Prior;
Mears, Warner, Wilkins run: delusive thought!
Breval, Bond, Besaleel, the varlets caught.

Curl stretches after Gay, but Gay is gone,
He grasps an empty Joseph for a John:
So Proteus, hunted in a nobler shape,
Became, when seiz'd, a puppy, or an ape.
To him the Goddess: Son! thy grief lay down,
And turn this whole illusion on the town:
As the sage dame, experienc'd in her trade,
By names of Toasts retails each batter'd jade;
(Whence hapless Monsieur much complains at Paris
Of wrongs from Duchesses and Lady Maries;)
Be thine, my stationer! this magic gift;
Cook shall be Prior, and Concanen, Swift:
So shall each hostile name become our own,
And we too boast our Garth and Addison.
With that she gave him (piteous of his case,
Yet smiling at his rueful length of face)

A shaggy Tap'stry, worthy to be spread
On Codrus' old, or Dunton's modern bed;

Instructive work! whose wry–mouth'd portraiture
Display'd the fates her confessors endure.

Earless on high, stood unabash'd De Foe,
And Tutchin flagrant from the scourge below.
There Ridpath, Roper, cudgell'd might ye view,
The very worsted still look'd black and blue.
Himself among the story'd chiefs he spies,
As from the blanket high in air he flies,
And oh! (he cry'd) what street, what lane but knows,
Our purgings, pumpings, blankettings, and blows?

In ev'ry loom our labours shall be seen,
And the fresh vomit run for ever green!
See in the circle next, Eliza plac'd,
Two babes of love close clinging to her waist;
Fair as before her works she stands confess'd,
In flow'rs and pearls by bounteous Kirkall dress'd.

The Goddess then: "Who best can send on high
"The salient spout, far–streaming to the sky;
"His be yon Juno of majestic size,
"With cow–like udders, and with ox–like eyes.
"This China Jordan let the chief o'ercome
"Replenish, not ingloriously, at home."
Osborne and Curl accept the glorious strife,
(Tho' this his Son dissuades, and that his Wife.)

One on his manly confidence relies,
One on his vigour and superior size.
First Osborne lean'd against his letter'd post;
It rose, and labour'd to a curve at most.
So Jove's bright bow displays its wat'ry round,
(Sure sign, that no spectator shall be drown'd)
A second effort brought but new disgrace,
The wild Meander wash'd the Artist's face:
Thus the small jett, which hasty hands unlock,
Spirts in the gard'ner's eyes who turns the cock.
Not so from shameless Curl; impetuous spread
The stream, and smoking flourish'd o'er his head.
So (fam'd like thee for turbulence and horns)
Eridanus his humble fountain scorns;

Thro' half the heav'ns he pours th'exalted urn;
His rapid waters in their passage burn.
Swift as it mounts, all follow with their eyes:
Still happy Impudence obtains the prize.

Thou triumph'st, Victor of the high–wrought day,
And the pleas'd dame, soft–smiling, lead'st away.
Osborne, thro' perfect modesty o'ercome,
Crown'd with the Jordan, walks contented home.
But now for Authors nobler palms remain;
Room for my Lord! three jockeys in his train;
Six huntsmen with a shout precede his chair:
He grins, and looks broad nonsense with a stare.
His Honour's meaning Dulness thus exprest,
"He wins this Patron, who can tickle best."
He chinks his purse, and takes his seat of state:
With ready quills the Dedicators wait;

Now at his head the dextrous task commence,
And, instant, fancy feels th'imputed sense;
Now gentle touches wanton o'er his face,
He struts Adonis, and affects grimace:
Rolli the feather to his ear conveys,
Then his nice taste directs our Operas:
Bentley his mouth with classic flatt'ry opes,
And the puff'd orator bursts out in tropes.

But Welsted most the Poet's healing balm
Strives to extract from his soft, giving palm;
Unlucky Welsted! thy unfeeling master,
The more thou ticklest, gripes his fist the faster.
While thus each hand promotes the pleasing pain,
And quick sensations skip from vein to vein;

A youth unknown to Phoebus, in despair,
Puts his last refuge all in heav'n and pray'r.
What force have pious vows! The Queen of Love
His sister sends, her vot'ress, from above.
As taught by Venus, Paris learnt the art
To touch Achilles' only tender part;
Secure, thro' her, the noble prize to carry,

He marches off, his Grace's Secretary.
Now turn to diff'rent sports (the Goddess cries)
And learn, my sons, the wond'rous pow'r of Noise.
To move, to raise, to ravish ev'ry heart,
With Shakespear's nature, or with Johnson's art,
Let others aim: 'Tis yours to shake the soul
With Thunder rumbling from the mustard bowl,

With horns and trumpets now to madness swell,
Now sink in sorrows with a tolling bell;
Such happy arts attention can command,
When fancy flags, and sense is at a stand.
Improve we these. Three Cat–calls be the bribe
Of him, whose chatt'ring shames the Monkey tribe:
And his this Drum, whose hoarse heroic base
Drowns the loud clarion of the braying Ass.
Now thousand tongues are heard in one loud din:
The Monkey–mimics rush discordant in;
'Twas chatt'ring, grinning, mouthing, jabb'ring all,
And Noise and Norton, Brangling and Breval,
Dennis and Dissonance, and captious Art,
And Snip–snap short, and Interruption smart,
And Demonstration thin, and Theses thick,
And Major, Minor, and Conclusion quick.
Hold (cry'd the Queen) a Cat–call each shall win;
Equal your merits! equal is your din!

But that this well–disputed game may end,
Sound forth my Brayers, and the welkin rend.
As when the long–ear'd milky mothers wait
At some sick miser's triple–bolted gate,
For their defrauded, absent foals they make
A moan so loud, that all the guild awake;
Sore sighs Sir Gilbert, starting at the bray,
From dreams of millions, and three groats to pay.
So swells each wind–pipe; Ass intones to Ass,

Harmonic twang! of leather, horn, and brass;
Such as from lab'ring lungs th'Enthusiast blows,
High Sound, attemp'red to the vocal nose;
Or such as bellow from the deep Divine;
There Webster! peal'd thy voice, and Whitfield! thine.
But far o'er all, sonorous Blackmore's strain;
Walls, steeples, skies, bray back to him again.

In Tot'nam fields, the brethren with amaze
Prick all their ears up, and forget to graze;
Long Chanc'ry–lane retentive rolls the sound,
And courts to courts return it round and round;
Thames wafts it thence to Rufus' roaring hall,
And Hungerford re–echoes bawl for bawl.
All hail him victor in both gifts of song,
Who sings so loudly, and who sings so long.
This labour past, by Bridewell all descend,
(As morning pray'r, and flagellation end)

To where Fleet–ditch with disemboguing streams
Rolls the large tribute of dead dogs to Thames,
The King of dykes! than whom no sluice of mud
With deeper sable blots the silver flood.
"Here strip, my children! here at once leap in,
"Here prove who best can dash thro' thick and thin,
"And who the most in love of dirt excel,
"Or dark dexterity of groping well.

"Who flings most filth, and wide pollutes around
"The stream, be his the Weekly Journals bound,
"A pig of lead to him who dives the best;
"A peck of coals a–piece shall glad the rest."
In naked majesty Oldmixon stands,
And Milo–like surveys his arms and hands;

Then sighing, thus, "And am I now three–score?

"Ah why, ye Gods! should two and two make four?"
He said, and clim'd a stranded lighter's height,
Shot to the black abyss, and plung'd down–right.
The Senior's judgment all the crowd admire,
Who but to sink the deeper, rose the higher.
Next Smedley div'd; slow circles dimpled o'er
The quaking mud, that clos'd, and op'd no more.

All look, all sigh, and call on Smedley lost;
Smedley in vain resounds thro' all the coast.
Then — essay'd; scarce vanish'd out of sight,
He buoys up instant, and returns to light:
He bears no token of the sabler streams,
And mounts far off among the Swans of Thames.
True to the bottom, see Concanen creep,
A cold, long–winded, native of the deep:
If perseverance gain the Diver's prize,
Not everlasting Blackmore this denies:

No noise, no stir, no motion can'st thou make,
Th'unconscious stream sleeps o'er thee like a lake.
Next plung'd a feeble, but a desp'rate pack,
With each a sickly brother at his back:
Sons of a Day! just buoyant on the flood,
Then number'd with the puppies in the mud.
Ask ye their names? I could as soon disclose
The names of these blind puppies as of those.
Fast by, like Niobe (her children gone)
Sits Mother Osborne, stupify'd to stone!
And Monumental Brass this record bears,
"These are,—ah no! these were, the Gazetteers!"
Not so bold Arnall; with a weight of skull,
Furious he dives, precipitately dull.
Whirlpools and storms his circling arm invest,
With all the might of gravitation blest.
No crab more active in the dirty dance,

Downward to climb, and backward to advance.

He brings up half the bottom on his head,
And loudly claims the Journals and the Lead.
The plunging Prelate, and his pond'rous Grace,
With holy envy gave one Layman place.
When lo! a burst of thunder shook the flood.
Slow rose a form, in majesty of Mud;
Shaking the horrors of his sable brows,
And each ferocious feature grim with ooze.
Greater he looks, and more than mortal stares:
Then thus the wonders of the deep declares.
First he relates, how sinking to the chin,
Smit with his mien, the Mud–nymphs suck'd him in:
How young Lutetia, softer than the down,
Nigrina black, and Merdamante brown,
Vy'd for his love in jetty bow'rs below,
As Hylas fair was ravish'd long ago.
Then sung, how shown him by the Nut–brown maids
A branch of Styx here rises from the Shades,

That tinctur'd as it runs with Lethe's streams,
And wasting Vapours from the Land of dreams,
(As under seas Alphæus' secret sluice
Bears Pisa's off'rings to his Arethuse)
Pours into Thames: and hence the mingled wave
Intoxicates the pert, and lulls the grave:
Here brisker vapours o'er the Temple creep,
There, all from Paul's to Aldgate drink and sleep.
Thence to the banks where rev'rend Bards repose,
They led him soft; each rev'rend Bard arose;

And Milbourn chief, deputed by the rest,
Gave him the cassock, surcingle, and vest.
"Receive (he said) these robes which once were mine,
"Dulness is sacred in a sound divine."

He ceas'd, and spread the robe; the crowd confess
The rev'rend Flamen in his lengthen'd dress.
Around him wide a sable Army stand,
A low–born, cell–bred, selfish, servile band,
Prompt or to guard or stab, to saint or damn,
Heav'n's Swiss, who fight for any God, or Man.
Thro' Lud's fam'd gates, along the well–known Fleet
Rolls the black troop, and overshades the street,
'Till show'rs of Sermons, Characters, Essays,
In circling fleeces whiten all the ways:
So clouds replenish'd from some bog below,
Mount in dark volumes, and descend in snow.
Here stopt the Goddess; and in pomp proclaims
A gentler exercise to close the games.
"Ye Critics! in whose heads, as equal scales,
"I weigh what author's heaviness prevails;
"Which most conduce to sooth the soul in slumbers,
"My H—ley's periods, or my Blackmore's numbers;
"Attend the trial we propose to make:
"If there be man, who o'er such works can wake,
"Sleep's all–subduing charms who dares defy,
"And boasts Ulysses' ear with Argus' eye;
"To him we grant our amplest pow'rs to sit
"Judge of all present, past, and future wit;

"To cavil, censure, dictate, right or wrong,
"Full and eternal privilege of tongue."
Three College Sophs, and three pert Templars came,
The same their talents, and their tastes the same;
Each prompt to query, answer, and debate,
And smit with love of Poesy and Prate.
The pond'rous books two gentle readers bring;
The heroes sit, the vulgar form a ring.
The clam'rous crowd is hush'd with mugs of Mum,
'Till all tun'd equal, send a gen'ral hum.
Then mount the Clerks, and in one lazy tone

Thro' the long, heavy, painful page drawl on;
Soft creeping, words on words, the sense compose,
At ev'ry line they stretch, they yawn, they doze.

As to soft gales top–heavy pines bow low
Their heads, and lift them as they cease to blow:
Thus oft they rear, and oft the head decline,
As breathe, or pause, by fits, the airs divine.
And now to this side, now to that they nod,
As verse, or prose, infuse the drowzy God.
Thrice Budgel aim'd to speak, but thrice supprest
By potent Arthur, knock'd his chin and breast.
Toland and Tindal, prompt at priests to jeer,
Yet silent bow'd to Christ's No kingdom here.
Who sate the nearest, by the words o'ercome,
Slept first; the distant nodded to the hum.
Then down are roll'd the books; stretch'd o'er 'em lies
Each gentle clerk, and mutt'ring seals his eyes.
As what a Dutchman plumps into the lakes,
One circle first, and then a second makes;

What Dulness dropt among her sons imprest
Like motion from one circle to the rest;
So from the mid–most the nutation spreads
Round and more round, o'er all the sea of heads.
At last Centlivre felt her voice to fail,
Motteux himself unfinish'd left his tale,
Boyer the State, and Law the Stage gave o'er,
Morgan and Mandevil could prate no more;

Norton, from Daniel and Ostroea sprung,
Bless'd with his father's front, and mother's tongue,
Hung silent down his never–blushing head;
And all was hush'd, as Folly's self lay dead.
Thus the soft gifts of Sleep conclude the day,
And stretch'd on bulks, as usual, Poets lay.

Why should I sing what bards the nightly Muse
Did slumb'ring visit, and convey to stews;
Who prouder march'd, with magistrates in state,
To some fam'd round–house, ever open gate!
How Henley lay inspir'd beside a sink,
And to mere mortals seem'd a Priest in drink:
While others, timely, to the neighb'ring Fleet
(Haunt of the Muses) made their safe retreat. The End of the Second Book.

Book the Third.

ARGUMENT.

After the other persons are disposed in their proper places of rest, the Goddess transports the King to her Temple, and there lays him to slumber with his head on her lap; a position of marvellous virtue, which causes all the Visions of wild enthusiasts, projectors, politicians, inamoratos, castle–builders, chemists, and poets. He is immediately carried on the wings of Fancy, and led by a mad Poetical Sibyl, to the Elysian shade; where, on the banks of Lethe, the souls of the dull are dipped by Bavius, before their entrance into this world. There he is met by the ghost of Settle, and by him made acquainted with the wonders of the place, and with those which he himself is destined to perform. He takes him to a Mount of Vision, from whence he shews him the past triumphs of the Empire of Dulness, then the present, and lastly the future: how small a part of the world was ever conquered by Science, how soon those conquests were stopped, and those very nations again reduced to her dominion. Then distinguishing the Island of Great–Britain, shews by what aids, by what persons, and by what degrees it shall be brought to her Empire. Some of the persons he causes to pass in review before his eyes, describing each by his proper figure, character, and qualifications. On a sudden the Scene shifts, and a vast number of miracles and prodigies appear, utterly surprising and unknown to the King himself, 'till they are explained to be the wonders of his own reign now commencing. On this Subject Settle breaks into a congratulation, yet not unmixed with concern, that his own times were but the types of these. He prophesies how first the nation shall be over–run with Farces, Operas, and Shows; how the throne of Dulness shall be advanced over the Theatres, and set up even at Court: then how her Sons shall preside in the seats of Arts and Sciences: giving a glimpse, or Pisgah–sight of the future Fulness of her Glory, the accomplishment whereof is the subject of the fourth and last book.

But in her Temple's last recess inclos'd,
On Dulness' lap th'Anointed head repos'd.
Him close she curtains round with Vapours blue,
And soft besprinkles with Cimmerian dew.
Then raptures high the seat of Sense o'erflow,
Which only heads refin'd from Reason know.
Hence, from the straw where Bedlam's Prophet nods,
He hears loud Oracles, and talks with Gods:
Hence the Fool's Paradise, the Statesman's Scheme,
The air–built Castle, and the golden Dream,
The Maid's romantic wish, the Chemist's flame,
And Poet's vision of eternal Fame.
And now, on Fancy's easy wing convey'd,
The King descending, views th'Elysian Shade.

A slip–shod Sibyl led his steps along,
In lofty madness meditating song;
Her tresses staring from Poetic dreams,
And never wash'd, but in Castalia's streams.
Taylor, their better Charon, lends an oar,
(Once swan of Thames, tho' now he sings no more.)
Benlowes, propitious still to blockheads, bows;
And Shadwell nods the Poppy on his brows.

Here, in a dusky vale where Lethe rolls,
Old Bavius sits, to dip poetic souls,
And blunt the sense, and fit it for a skull
Of solid proof, impenetrably dull:
Instant, when dipt, away they wing their flight,

Where Brown and Mears unbar the gates of Light,

Demand new bodies, and in Calf's array,
Rush to the world, impatient for the day.
Millions and millions on these banks he views,
Thick as the stars of night, or morning dews,
As thick as bees o'er vernal blossoms fly,
As thick as eggs at Ward in Pillory.
Wond'ring he gaz'd: When lo! a Sage appears,
By his broad shoulders known, and length of ears,

Known by the band and suit which Settle wore
(His only suit) for twice three years before:
All as the vest, appear'd the wearer's frame,
Old in new state, another yet the same.
Bland and familiar as in life, begun
Thus the great Father to the greater Son.
Oh born to see what none can see awake!
Behold the wonders of th'oblivious Lake.
Thou, yet unborn, hast touch'd this sacred shore;
The hand of Bavius drench'd thee o'er and o'er.
But blind to former as to future fate,
What mortal knows his pre–existent state?
Who knows how long thy transmigrating soul
Might from Boeotian to Boeotian roll?
How many Dutchmen she vouchsaf'd to thrid?
How many stages thro' old Monks she rid?
And all who since, in mild benighted days,
Mix'd the Owl's ivy with the Poet's bays.
As man's Mæanders to the vital spring
Roll all their tides, then back their circles bring;
Or whirligigs, twirl'd round by skilful swain,
Suck the thread in, then yield it out again:
All nonsense thus, of old or modern date,
Shall in thee centre, from thee circulate.

For this our Queen unfolds to vision true
Thy mental eye, for thou hast much to view:
Old scenes of glory, times long cast behind
Shall, first recall'd, rush forward to thy mind:
Then stretch thy sight o'er all her rising reign,
And let the past and future fire thy brain.
Ascend this hill, whose cloudy point commands
Her boundless empire over seas and lands.
See, round the Poles where keener spangles shine,
Where spices smoke beneath the burning Line,
(Earth's wide extremes) her sable flag display'd,
And all the nations cover'd in her shade!
Far eastward cast thine eye, from whence the Sun
And orient Science their bright course begun:
One god–like Monarch all that pride confounds,
He, whose long wall the wand'ring Tartar bounds;
Heav'ns! what a pile! whole ages perish there,
And one bright blaze turns Learning into air.
Thence to the south extend thy gladden'd eyes;
There rival flames with equal glory rise,
From shelves to shelves see greedy Vulcan roll,
And lick up all their Physic of the Soul.
How little, mark! that portion of the ball,
Where, faint at best, the beams of Science fall:
Soon as they dawn, from Hyperborean skies
Embody'd dark, what clouds of Vandals rise!
Lo! where Mæotis sleeps, and hardly flows
The freezing Tanais thro' a waste of snows,
The North by myriads pours her mighty sons,
Great nurse of Goths, of Alans, and of Huns!
See Alaric's stern port! the martial frame
Of Genseric! and Attila's dread name!

See the bold Ostrogoths on Latium fall;
See the fierce Visigoths on Spain and Gaul!
See, where the morning gilds the palmy shore

(The soil that arts and infant letters bore)
His conqu'ring tribes th'Arabian prophet draws,
And saving Ignorance enthrones by Laws.
See Christians, Jews, one heavy sabbath keep,
And all the western world believe and sleep.
Lo! Rome herself, proud mistress now no more
Of arts, but thund'ring against heathen lore;
Her grey–hair'd Synods damning books unread,
And Bacon trembling for his brazen head.

Padua, with sighs, beholds her Livy burn,
And ev'n th'Antipodes Vigilius mourn.
See, the Cirque falls, th'unpillar'd Temple nods,
Streets pav'd with Heroes, Tyber choak'd with Gods:
'Till Peter's keys some christ'ned Jove adorn,
And Pan to Moses lends his pagan horn;
See graceless Venus to a Virgin turn'd,
Or Phidias broken, and Apelles burn'd.
Behold yon' Isle, by Palmers, Pilgrims trod,
Men bearded, bald, cowl'd, uncowl'd, shod, unshod,
Peel'd, patch'd, and pyebald, linsey–wolsey brothers,
Grave Mummers! sleeveless some, and shirtless others.
That once was Britain—Happy! had she seen
No fiercer sons, had Easter never been.

In peace, great Goddess, ever be ador'd;
How keen the war, if Dulness draw the sword!
Thus visit not thy own! on this blest age
Oh spread thy Influence, but restrain thy Rage.
And see, my son! the hour is on its way,
That lifts our Goddess to imperial sway;
This fav'rite Isle, long sever'd from her reign,
Dove–like, she gathers to her wings again.
Now look thro' Fate! behold the scene she draws!
What aids, what armies to assert her cause!
See all her progeny, illustrious sight!

Behold, and count them, as they rise to light.
As Berecynthia, while her offspring vye
In homage to the Mother of the sky,

Surveys around her, in the blest abode,
An hundred sons, and ev'ry son a God:
Not with less glory mighty Dulness crown'd,
Shall take thro' Grub–street her triumphant round;
And her Parnassus glancing o'er at once,
Behold an hundred sons, and each a Dunce.
Mark first that Youth who takes the foremost place,
And thrusts his person full into your face.
With all thy Father's virtues blest, be born!
And a new Cibber shall the stage adorn.
A second see, by meeker manners known,
And modest as the maid that sips alone;

From the strong fate of drams if thou get free,
Another Durfey, Ward! shall sing in thee.
Thee shall each ale–house, thee each gill–house mourn,
And answ'ring gin–shops sowrer sighs return.
Jacob, the scourge of Grammar, mark with awe,
Nor less revere him, blunderbuss of Law.

Lo P—p—le's brow, tremendous to the town,
Horneck's fierce eye, and Roome's funereal Frown.
Lo sneering Goode, half malice and half whim,
A Fiend in glee, ridiculously grim.
Each Cygnet sweet of Bath and Tunbridge race,
Whose tuneful whistling makes the waters pass:
Each Songster, Riddler, ev'ry nameless name,
All crowd, who foremost shall be damn'd to Fame.
Some strain in rhyme; the Muses, on their racks,
Scream like the winding of ten thousand jacks:

Some free from rhyme or reason, rule or check,

Break Priscian's head, and Pegasus's neck;
Down, down they larum, with impetuous whirl,
The Pindars, and the Miltons of a Curl.
Silence, ye Wolves! while Ralph to Cynthia howls,
And makes Night hideous—Answer him, ye Owls!
Sense, speech, and measure, living tongues and dead,
Let all give way—and Morris may be read.
Flow Welsted, flow! like thine inspirer, Beer,
Tho' stale, not ripe; tho' thin, yet never clear;

So sweetly mawkish, and so smoothly dull;
Heady, not strong; o'erflowing, tho' not full.
Ah Dennis! Gildon ah! what ill–starr'd rage
Divides a friendship long confirm'd by age?
Blockheads with reason wicked wits abhor,
But fool with fool is barb'rous civil war.
Embrace, embrace my sons! be foes no more!
Nor glad vile Poets with true Critics gore.
Behold yon Pair, in strict embraces join'd;
How like in manners, and how like in mind!

Equal in wit, and equally polite,
Shall this a Pasquin, that a Grumbler write;
Like are their merits, like rewards they share,
That shines a Consul, this Commissioner.
"But who is he, in closet close y–pent,
"Of sober face, with learned dust besprent?
Right well mine eyes arede the myster wight,
On parchment scraps y–fed, and Wormius hight.

To future ages may thy dulness last,
As thou preserv'st the dulness of the past!
There, dim in clouds, the poring Scholiasts mark,
Wits, who like owls, see only in the dark,

A Lumberhouse of books in ev'ry head,

For ever reading, never to be read!
But, where each Science lifts its modern type,
Hist'ry her Pot, Divinity her Pipe,
While proud Philosophy repines to show,
Dishonest sight! his breeches rent below;
Imbrown'd with native bronze, lo! Henley stands,
Tuning his voice, and balancing his hands.

How fluent nonsense trickles from his tongue!
How sweet the periods, neither said, nor sung!
Still break the benches, Henley! with thy strain,
While Sherlock, Hare, and Gibson preach in vain.
Oh great Restorer of the good old Stage,
Preacher at once, and Zany of thy age!
Oh worthy thou of Ægypt's wise abodes,
A decent priest, where monkeys were the gods!
But fate with butchers plac'd thy priestly stall,
Meek modern faith to murder, hack, and mawl;
And bade thee live, to crown Britannia's praise,
In Toland's, Tindal's, and in Woolston's days.
Yet oh, my sons! a father's words attend:
(So may the fates preserve the ears you lend)

'Tis yours, a Bacon or a Locke to blame,
A Newton's genius, or a Milton's flame:
But oh! with One, immortal one dispense,
The source of Newton's Light, of Bacon's Sense!
Content, each Emanation of his fires
That beams on earth, each Virtue he inspires,
Each Art he prompts, each Charm he can create,
Whate'er he gives, are giv'n for you to hate.
Persist, by all divine in Man unaw'd,
But, "Learn, ye Dunces! not to scorn your God."
Thus he, for then a ray of Reason stole
Half thro' the solid darkness of his soul;
But soon the cloud return'd—and thus the Sire:

See now, what Dulness and her sons admire!
See what the charms, that smite the simple heart
Not touch'd by Nature, and not reach'd by Art.
His never–blushing head he turn'd aside,
(Not half so pleas'd when Goodman prophesy'd)

And look'd, and saw a sable Sorc'rer rise,
Swift to whose hand a winged volume flies:
All sudden, Gorgons hiss, and Dragons glare,
And ten–horn'd fiends and Giants rush to war.
Hell rises, Heav'n descends, and dance on Earth:
Gods, imps, and monsters, music, rage, and mirth,
A fire, a jigg, a battle, and a ball,
'Till one wide conflagration swallows all.
Thence a new world to Nature's laws unknown,
Breaks out refulgent, with a heav'n its own:
Another Cynthia her new journey runs,
And other planets circle other suns.
The forests dance, the rivers upward rise,
Whales sport in woods, and dolphins in the skies;

And last, to give the whole creation grace,
Lo! one vast Egg produces human race.
Joy fills his soul, joy innocent of thought;
What pow'r, he cries, what pow'r these wonders wrought?
Son; what thou seek'st is in thee! Look, and find
Each Monster meets his likeness in thy mind.
Yet would'st thou more? In yonder cloud behold,
Whose sarsenet skirts are edg'd with flamy gold,
A matchless Youth! his nod these worlds controuls,
Wings the red lightning, and the thunder rolls.
Angel of Dulness, sent to scatter round
Her magic charms o'er all unclassic ground:
Yon stars, yon suns, he rears at pleasure higher,
Illumes their light, and sets their flames on fire.
Immortal Rich! how calm he sits at ease

'Mid snows of paper, and fierce hail of pease;

And proud his Mistress' orders to perform,
Rides in the whirlwind, and directs the storm.
But lo! to dark encounter in mid air
New wizards rise; I see my Cibber there!
Booth in his cloudy tabernacle shrin'd,
On grinning dragons thou shalt mount the wind.

Dire is the conflict, dismal is the din,
Here shouts all Drury, there all Lincoln's–inn;
Contending Theatres our empire raise,
Alike their labours, and alike their praise.
And are these wonders, Son, to thee unknown?
Unknown to thee? These wonders are thy own.
These Fate reserv'd to grace thy reign divine,
Foreseen by me, but ah! with–held from mine.
In Lud's old walls tho' long I rul'd, renown'd
Far as loud Bow's stupendous bells resound;
Tho' my own Aldermen confer'd the bays,
To me committing their eternal praise,
Their full–fed Heroes, their pacific May'rs,
Their annual trophies, and their monthly wars:
Tho' long my Party built on me their hopes,
For writing Pamphlets, and for roasting Popes;
Yet lo! in me what authors have to brag on!
Reduc'd at last to hiss in my own dragon.
Avert it Heav'n! that thou, my Cibber, e'er
Should'st wag a serpent–tail in Smithfield fair!

Like the vile straw that's blown about the streets,
The needy Poet sticks to all he meets,
Coach'd, carted, trod upon, now loose, now fast,
And carry'd off in some Dog's tail at last.
Happier thy fortunes! like a rolling stone,
Thy giddy dulness still shall lumber on,

Safe in its heaviness, shall never stray,
But lick up ev'ry blockhead in the way.
Thee shall the Patriot, thee the Courtier taste,
And ev'ry year be duller than the last.
'Till rais'd from booths, to Theatre, to Court,
Her seat imperial Dulness shall transport.
Already Opera prepares the way,
The sure fore–runner of her gentle sway:
Let her thy heart, next Drabs and Dice, engage,
The third mad passion of thy doting age.

Teach thou the warb'ling Polypheme to roar,
And scream thyself as none e'er scream'd before!
To aid our cause, if Heav'n thou can'st not bend,
Hell thou shalt move; for Faustus is our friend:
Pluto with Cato thou for this shalt join,
And link the Mourning Bride to Proserpine.
Grubstreet! thy fall should men and Gods conspire,
Thy stage shall stand, ensure it but from Fire.
Another Æschylus appears! prepare
For new abortions, all ye pregnant fair!
In flames, like Semele's, be brought to bed,
While op'ning Hell spouts wild–fire at your head.
Now Bavius take the poppy from thy brow,
And place it here! here all ye Heroes bow!
This, this is he, foretold by ancient rhymes:
Th'Augustus born to bring Saturnian times.
Signs following signs lead on the mighty year!
See! the dull stars roll round and re–appear.
See, see, our own true Phoebus wears the bays!
Our Midas sits Lord Chancellor of Plays!
On Poets Tombs see Benson's titles writ!
Lo! Ambrose Philips is prefer'd for Wit!

See under Ripley rise a new White–hall,
While Jones' and Boyle's united labours fall:

While Wren with sorrow to the grave descends,
Gay dies unpension'd with a hundred friends,

Hibernian Politics, O Swift! thy fate;
And Pope's, ten years to comment and translate.
Proceed, great days! 'till Learning fly the shore,
'Till Birch shall blush with noble blood no more,
'Till Thames see Eaton's sons for ever play,
'Till Westminster's whole year be holiday,

'Till Isis' Elders reel, their pupils sport,
And Alma mater lie dissolv'd in Port!
Enough! enough! the raptur'd Monarch cries;
And thro' the Iv'ry Gate the Vision flies. The End of the Third Book.

Book the Fourth.

ARGUMENT.

The Poet being, in this Book, to declare the Completion of the Prophecies mention'd at the end of the former, makes a new Invocation; as the greater Poets are wont, when some high and worthy matter is to be sung. He shews the Goddess coming in her Majesty, to destroy Order and Science, and to substitute the Kingdom of the Dull upon earth. How she leads captive the Sciences, and silenceth the Muses; and what they be who succeed in their stead. All her Children, by a wonderful attraction, are drawn about her; and bear along with them divers others, who promote her Empire by connivance, weak resistance, or discouragement of Arts; such as Half–wits, tasteless Admirers, vain Pretenders, the Flatterers of Dunces, or the Patrons of them. All these crowd round her; one of them offering to approach her, is driven back by a Rival, but she commends and encourages both. The first who speak in form are the Genius's of the Schools, who assure her of their care to advance her Cause, by confining Youth to Words, and keeping them out of the way of real Knowledge. Their Address, and her gracious Answer; with her Charge to

them and the Universities. The Universities appear by their proper Deputies, and assure her that the same method is observ'd in the progress of Education; The speech of Aristarchus
on this subject. They are driven off by a band of young Gentlemen return'd from Travel with their Tutors; one of whom delivers to the Goddess, in a polite oration, an account of the whole Conduct and Fruits of their Travels: presenting to her at the same time a young Nobleman perfectly accomplished. She receives him graciously, and indues him with the happy quality of Want of Shame. She sees loitering about her a number of Indolent Persons abandoning all business and duty, and dying with laziness: To these approaches the Antiquary Annius, intreating her to make them Virtuosos, and assign them over to him: But Mummius, another Antiquary, complaining of his fraudulent proceeding, she finds a method to reconcile their difference. Then enter a Troop of people fantastically adorn'd, offering her strange and exotic presents: Amongst them, one stands forth and demands justice on another, who had deprived him of one of the greatest Curiosities in nature: but he justifies himself so well, that the Goddess gives them both her approbation. She recommends to them to find proper employment for the Indolents before–mentioned, in the study of Butterflies, Shells, Birds–nests, Moss, &c. but with particular caution, not to proceed beyond Trifles, to any useful or extensive views of Nature, or of the Author of Nature. Against the last of these apprehensions, she is secured by a hearty Address from the Minute Philosophers and Freethinkers, one of whom speaks in the name of the rest. The Youth thus instructed and principled, are delivered to her in a body, by the hands of Silenus; and then admitted to taste the Cup of the Magus her High Priest, which causes a total oblivion of all Obligations, divine, civil, moral, or rational. To these her Adepts she sends Priests, Attendants, and Comforters, of various kinds; confers on them Orders and Degrees; and then dismissing them with a speech, confirming to each his Privileges and telling what she expects from each, concludes with a Yawn of extraordinary virtue: The Progress and Effects whereof on all Orders of men, and the Consummation of all, in the Restoration of Night and Chaos, conclude the Poem.

Yet, yet a moment, one dim Ray of Light
Indulge, dread Chaos, and eternal Night!
Of darkness visible so much be lent,
As half to shew, half veil the deep Intent.
Ye Pow'rs! whose Mysteries restor'd I sing,
To whom Time bears me on his rapid wing,

Suspend a while your Force inertly strong,
Then take at once the Poet and the Song.
Now flam'd the Dog–star's unpropitious ray,
Smote ev'ry Brain, and wither'd ev'ry Bay;
Sick was the Sun, the Owl forsook his bow'r,
The moon–struck Prophet felt the madding hour:
Then rose the Seed of Chaos, and of Night,
To blot out Order, and extinguish Light,
Of dull and venal a new World to mold,
And bring Saturnian days of Lead and Gold.
She mounts the Throne: her head a Cloud conceal'd,
In broad Effulgence all below reveal'd,
('Tis thus aspiring Dulness ever shines)
Soft on her lap her Laureat son reclines.
Beneath her foot–stool, *Science* groans in Chains,
And *Wit* dreads Exile, Penalties and Pains.

There foam'd rebellious *Logic*, gagg'd and bound,
There, stript, fair *Rhet'ric* languish'd on the ground;
His blunted Arms by *Sophistry* are born,
And shameless *Billingsgate* her Robes adorn.
Morality, by her false Guardians drawn,
Chicane in Furs, and *Casuistry* in Lawn,
Gasps, as they straiten at each end the cord,
And dies, when Dulness gives her Page the word.
Mad *Mathesis* alone was unconfin'd,
Too mad for mere material chains to bind,

Now to pure Space lifts her extatic stare,
Now running round the Circle, finds it square.
But held in ten–fold bonds the *Muses* lie,
Watch'd both by Envy's and by Flatt'ry's eye:
There to her heart sad Tragedy addrest
The dagger wont to pierce the Tyrant's breast;
But sober History restrain'd her rage,

And promis'd Vengeance on a barb'rous age.
There sunk Thalia, nerveless, cold, and dead,
Had not her Sister Satyr held her head:

Nor cou'd'st thou, Chesterfield! a tear refuse,
Thou wept'st, and with thee wept each gentle Muse.
When lo! a Harlot form soft sliding by,
With mincing step, small voice, and languid eye;
Foreign her air, her robe's discordant pride
In patch–work flutt'ring, and her head aside:
By singing Peers up–held on either hand,
She tripp'd and laugh'd, too pretty much to stand;
Cast on the prostrate Nine a scornful look,
Then thus in quaint Recitativo spoke.
O *Cara! Cara!* silence all that train:
Joy to great Chaos! let Division reign:

Chromatic tortures soon shall drive them hence,
Break all their nerves, and fritter all their sense:
One Trill shall harmonize joy, grief, and rage,
Wake the dull Church, and lull the ranting Stage;
To the same notes thy sons shall hum, or snore,
And all thy yawning daughters cry, *encore*.
Another Phoebus, thy own Phoebus, reigns,
Joys in my jiggs, and dances in my chains.
But soon, ah soon Rebellion will commence,
If Music meanly borrows aid from Sense:
Strong in new Arms, lo! Giant Handel stands,
Like bold Briareus, with a hundred hands;
To stir, to rouze, to shake the Soul he comes,
And Jove's own Thunders follow Mars's Drums.

Arrest him, Empress; or you sleep no more—
She heard, and drove him to th'Hibernian shore.
And now had Fame's posterior Trumpet blown,
And all the Nations summon'd to the Throne.

The young, the old, who feel her inward sway,
One instinct seizes, and transports away.
None need a guide, by sure Attraction led,
And strong impulsive gravity of Head:
None want a place, for all their Centre found,
Hung to the Goddess, and coher'd around.

Not closer, orb in orb, conglob'd are seen
The buzzing Bees about their dusky Queen.
The gath'ring number, as it moves along,
Involves a vast involuntary throng,
Who gently drawn, and struggling less and less,
Roll in her Vortex, and her pow'r confess.
Not those alone who passive own her laws,
But who, weak rebels, more advance her cause.
Whate'er of dunce in College or in Town
Sneers at another, in toupee or gown;
Whate'er of mungril no one class admits,
A wit with dunces, and a dunce with wits.
Nor absent they, no members of her state,
Who pay her homage in her sons, the Great;
Who false to Phoebus, bow the knee to Baal;
Or impious, preach his Word without a call.

Patrons, who sneak from living worth to dead,
With–hold the pension, and set up the head;
Or vest dull Flatt'ry in the sacred Gown;
Or give from fool to fool the Laurel crown.
And (last and worst) with all the cant of wit,
Without the soul, the Muse's Hypocrit.
There march'd the bard and blockhead, side by side,
Who rhym'd for hire, and patroniz'd for pride.
Narcissus, prais'd with all a Parson's pow'r,
Look'd a white lilly sunk beneath a show'r.
There mov'd Montalto with superior air;
His stretch'd–out arm display'd a Volume fair;

Courtiers and Patriots in two ranks divide,
Thro' both he pass'd, and bow'd from side to side:
But as in graceful act, with awful eye
Compos'd he stood, bold Benson thrust him by:
On two unequal crutches propt he came,
Milton's on this, on that one Johnston's name.

The decent Knight retir'd with sober rage,
"What! no respect, he cry'd, for Shakespear's page
But (happy for him as the times went then)
Appear'd Apollo's May'r and Aldermen,
On whom three hundred gold–capt youths await,
To lug the pond'rous volume off in state.
When Dulness, smiling—"Thus revive the Wits!
But murder first, and mince them all to bits;
As erst Medea (cruel, so to save!)
A new Edition of old Æson gave.
Let standard–Authors, thus, like trophies born,
Appear more glorious as more hack'd and torn,
And you, my Critics! in the checquer'd shade,
Admire new light thro' holes yourselves have made.
Leave not a foot of verse, a foot of stone,
A Page, a Grave, that they can call their own;

But spread, my sons, your glory thin or thick,
On passive paper, or on solid brick.
So by each Bard an Alderman shall sit,
A heavy Lord shall hang at ev'ry Wit,
And while on Fame's triumphal Car they ride,
Some Slave of mine be pinion'd to their side.
Now crowds on crowds around the Goddess press,
Each eager to present the first Address.
Dunce scorning Dunce beholds the next advance,
But Fop shews Fop superior complaisance.
When lo! a Spectre rose, whose index–hand
Held forth the Virtue of the dreadful wand;

His beaver'd brow a birchen garland wears,
Dropping with Infant's blood, and Mother's tears.
O'er ev'ry vein a shudd'ring horror runs;
Eton and Winton shake thro' all their Sons.

All Flesh is humbled, Westminster's bold race
Shrink, and confess the Genius of the place:
The pale Boy–Senator yet tingling stands,
And holds his breeches close with both his hands.
Then thus. Since Man from beast by Words is known,
Words are Man's province, Words we teach alone.
When Reason doubtful, like the Samian letter,
Points him two ways, the narrower is the better.
Plac'd at the door of Learning, youth to guide,
We never suffer it to stand too wide.
To ask, to guess, to know, as they commence,
As Fancy opens the quick springs of Sense,
We ply the Memory, we load the brain,
Bind rebel Wit, and double chain on chain,

Confine the thought, to exercise the breath;
And keep them in the pale of Words till death.
Whate'er the talents, or howe'er design'd,
We hang one jingling padlock on the mind:
A Poet the first day, he dips his quill;
And what the last? a very Poet still.
Pity! the charm works only in our wall,
Lost, lost too soon in yonder House or Hall.
There truant Wyndham ev'ry Muse gave o'er,
There Talbot sunk, and was a Wit no more!
How sweet an Ovid, Murray was our boast!
How many Martials were in Pult'ney lost!
Else sure some Bard, to our eternal praise,
In twice ten thousand rhyming nights and days,
Had reach'd the Work, the All that mortal can;
And South beheld that Master–piece of Man.

Oh (cry'd the Goddess) for some pedant Reign!
Some gentle James, to bless the land again;

To stick the Doctor's Chair into the Throne,
Give law to Words, or war with Words alone,
Senates and Courts with Greek and Latin rule,
And turn the Council to a Grammar School!

For sure, if Dulness sees a grateful Day,
'Tis in the shade of Arbitrary Sway.
O! if my sons may learn one earthly thing,
Teach but that one, sufficient for a King;
That which my Priests, and mine alone, maintain,
Which as it dies, or lives, we fall, or reign:
May you, may Cam, and Isis preach it long!
"The Right Divine of Kings to govern wrong."
Prompt at the call, around the Goddess roll
Broad hats, and hoods, and caps, a sable shoal:
Thick and more thick the black blockade extends,
A hundred head of Aristotle's friends.
Nor wert thou, Isis! wanting to the day,
[Tho' Christ–church long kept prudishly away.]

Each staunch Polemic, stubborn as a rock,
Each fierce Logician, still expelling Locke,
Came whip and spur, and dash'd thro' thin and thick
On German Crouzaz, and Dutch Burgersdyck.
As many quit the streams that murm'ring fall
To lull the sons of Marg'ret and Clare–hall,
Where Bentley late tempestuous wont to sport
In troubled waters, but now sleeps in Port.
Before them march'd that awful Aristarch;
Plow'd was his front with many a deep Remark:
His Hat, which never vail'd to human pride,
Walker with rev'rence took, and lay'd aside.

Low bow'd the rest: He, kingly, did but nod;
So upright Quakers please both Man and God.
Mistress! dismiss that rabble from your throne:
Avaunt—is Aristarchus yet unknown?
Thy mighty Scholiast, whose unweary'd pains
Made Horace dull, and humbled Milton's strains.
Turn what they will to Verse, their toil is vain,
Critics like me shall make it Prose again.
Roman and Greek Grammarians! know your Better:
Author of something yet more great than Letter;
While tow'ring o'er your Alphabet, like Saul,
Stands our Digamma, and o'er–tops them all.

'Tis true, on Words is still our whole debate,
Disputes of *Me* or *Te*, of *aut* or *at* ,
To sound or sink in *cano*, O or A,
Or give up Cicero to C or K.
Let Freind affect to speak as Terence spoke,
And Alsop never but like Horace joke:
For me, what Virgil, Pliny may deny,
Manilius or Solinus shall supply:
For Attic Phrase in Plato let them seek,
I poach in Suidas for unlicens'd Greek.
In ancient Sense if any needs will deal,
Be sure I give them Fragments, not a Meal;
What Gellius or Stobæus hash'd before,
Or chew'd by blind old Scholiasts o'er and o'er.

The critic Eye, that microscope of Wit,
Sees hairs and pores, examines bit by bit:
How parts relate to parts, or they to whole,
The body's harmony, the beaming soul,
Are things which Kuster, Burman, Wasse shall see,
When Man's whole frame is obvious to a *Flea*.
Ah, think not, Mistress! more true Dulness lies
In Folly's Cap, than Wisdom's grave disguise.

Like buoys, that never sink into the flood,
On Learning's surface we but lie and nod.
Thine is the genuine head of many a house,
And much Divinity without a Νουσ .

Nor could a Barrow work on ev'ry block,
Nor has one Atterbury spoil'd the flock.
See! still thy own, the heavy Canon roll,
And Metaphysic smokes involve the Pole.

For thee we dim the eyes, and stuff the head
With all such reading as was never read:
For thee explain a thing till all men doubt it,
And write about it, Goddess, and about it:
So spins the silk–worm small its slender store,
And labours till it clouds itself all o'er.
What tho' we let some better sort of fool
Thrid ev'ry science, run thro' ev'ry school?
Never by tumbler thro' the hoops was shown
Such skill in passing all, and touching none.

He may indeed (if sober all this time)
Plague with Dispute, or persecute with Rhyme.
We only furnish what he cannot use,
Or wed to what he must divorce, a Muse:
Full in the midst of Euclid dip at once,
And petrify a Genius to a Dunce:
Or set on Metaphysic ground to prance,
Show all his paces, not a step advance.
With the same Cement, ever sure to bind,
We bring to one dead level ev'ry mind.
Then take him to devellop, if you can,
And hew the Block off, and get out the Man.
But wherefore waste I words? I see advance
Whore, Pupil, and lac'd Governor from France.

Walker! our hat—nor more he deign'd to say,
But, stern as Ajax' spectre, strode away.
In flow'd at once a gay embroider'd race,
And titt'ring push'd the Pedants off the place:
Some would have spoken, but the voice was drown'd
By the French horn, or by the op'ning hound.
The first came forwards, with as easy mien,
As if he saw St. James's and the Queen.
When thus th'attendant Orator begun.
Receive, great Empress! thy accomplish'd Son:
Thine from the birth, and sacred from the rod,
A dauntless infant! never scar'd with God.
The Sire saw, one by one, his Virtues wake:
The Mother begg'd the blessing of a Rake.

Thou gav'st that Ripeness, which so soon began,
And ceas'd so soon, he ne'er was Boy, nor Man.
Thro' School and College, thy kind cloud o'ercast,
Safe and unseen the young Æneas past:
Thence bursting glorious, all at once let down,
Stunn'd with his giddy Larum half the town.
Intrepid then, o'er seas and lands he flew:
Europe he saw, and Europe saw him too.
There all thy gifts and graces we display,
Thou, only thou, directing all our way!
To where the Seine, obsequious as she runs,
Pours at great Bourbon's feet her silken sons;
Or Tyber, now no longer Roman, rolls,
Vain of Italian Arts, Italian Souls:

To happy Convents, bosom'd deep in vines,
Where slumber Abbots, purple as their wines:
To Isles of fragrance, lilly–silver'd vales,
Diffusing languor in the panting gales:
To lands of singing, or of dancing slaves,
Love–whisp'ring woods, and lute–resounding waves.

But chief her shrine where naked Venus keeps,
And Cupids ride the Lyon of the Deeps;
Where, eas'd of Fleets, the Adriatic main
Wafts the smooth Eunuch and enamour'd swain.
Led by my hand, he saunter'd Europe round,
And gather'd ev'ry Vice on Christian ground;
Saw ev'ry Court, hear'd ev'ry King declare
His royal Sense, of Op'ra's or the Fair;
The Stews and Palace equally explor'd,
Intrigu'd with glory, and with spirit whor'd;
Try'd all *hors–d'oeuvres*, all *liqueurs* defin'd,
Judicious drank, and greatly–daring din'd;
Dropt the dull lumber of the Latin store,
Spoil'd his own language, and acquir'd no more;

All Classic learning lost on Classic ground;
And last turn'd *Air*, the Echo of a Sound!
See now, half–cur'd, and perfectly well–bred,
With nothing but a Solo in his head;
As much Estate, and Principle, and Wit,
As Jansen, Fleetwood, Cibber shall think fit;
Stol'n from a Duel, follow'd by a Nun,
And, if a Borough chuse him, not undone;
See, to my country happy I restore
This glorious Youth, and add one Venus more.
Her too receive (for her my soul adores)
So may the sons of sons of sons of whores,

Prop thine, O Empress! like each neighbour Throne,
And make a long Posterity thy own.
Pleas'd, she accepts the Hero, and the Dame,
Wraps in her Veil, and frees from sense of Shame.
Then look'd, and saw a lazy, lolling sort,
Unseen at Church, at Senate, or at Court,
Of ever–listless Loit'rers, that attend
No Cause, no Trust, no Duty, and no Friend.

Thee too, my Paridel! she mark'd thee there,
Stretch'd on the rack of a too easy chair,
And heard thy everlasting yawn confess
The Pains and Penalties of Idleness.
She pity'd! but her Pity only shed
Benigner influence on thy nodding head.
But Annius, crafty Seer, with ebon wand,
And well dissembled em'rald on his hand,
False as his Gems, and canker'd as his Coins,
Came, cramm'd with capon, from where Pollio dines.
Soft, as the wily Fox is seen to creep,
Where bask on sunny banks the simple sheep,
Walk round and round, now prying here, now there;
So he; but pious, whisper'd first his pray'r.
Grant, gracious Goddess! grant me still to cheat,
O may thy cloud still cover the deceit!
Thy choicer mists on this assembly shed,
But pour them thickest on the noble head.
So shall each youth, assisted by our eyes,
See other Cæsars, other Homers rise;
Thro' twilight ages hunt th'Athenian fowl,
Which Chalcis Gods, and mortals call an Owl,

Now see an Attys, now a Cecrops clear,
Nay, Mahomet! the Pigeon at thine ear;
Be rich in ancient brass, tho' not in gold,
And keep his Lares, tho' his house be sold;
To headless Phoebe his fair bride postpone,
Honour a Syrian Prince above his own;
Lord of an Otho, if I vouch it true;
Blest in one Niger, till he knows of two.
Mummius o'erheard him; Mummius, Fool–renown'd,
Who like his Cheops stinks above the ground,
Fierce as a startled Adder, swell'd, and said,
Rattling an ancient Sistrum at his head.
Speak'st thou of Syrian Princes? Traitor base!

Mine, Goddess! mine is all the horned race.
True, he had wit, to make their value rise;
From foolish Greeks to steal them, was as wise;
More glorious yet, from barb'rous hands to keep,
When Sallee Rovers chac'd him on the deep.
Then taught by Hermes, and divinely bold,
Down his own throat he risqu'd the Grecian gold;
Receiv'd each Demi–God, with pious care,
Deep in his Entrails—I rever'd them there,
I bought them, shrouded in that living shrine,
And, at their second birth, they issue mine.
Witness great Ammon! by whose horns I swore,
(Reply'd soft Annius) this our paunch before

Still bears them, faithful; and that thus I eat,
Is to refund the Medals with the meat.
To prove me, Goddess! clear of all design,
Bid me with Pollio sup, as well as dine:
There all the Learn'd shall at the labour stand,
And Douglas lend his soft, obstetric hand.
The Goddess smiling seem'd to give consent;
So back to Pollio, hand in hand, they went.
Then thick as Locusts black'ning all the ground,
A tribe, with weeds and shells fantastic crown'd,
Each with some wond'rous gift approach'd the Pow'r,
A Nest, a Toad, a Fungus, or a Flow'r.
But far the foremost, two, with earnest zeal,
And aspect ardent to the Throne appeal.
The first thus open'd: Hear thy suppliant's call,
Great Queen, and common Mother of us all!
Fair from its humble bed I rear'd this Flow'r,
Suckled, and chear'd, with air, and sun, and show'r,

Soft on the paper ruff its leaves I spread,
Bright with the gilded button tipt its head,
Then thron'd in glass, and nam'd it Caroline:

Each Maid cry'd, charming! and each Youth, divine!
Did Nature's pencil ever blend such rays,
Such vary'd light in one promiscuous blaze?
Now prostrate! dead! behold that Caroline:
No Maid cries, charming! and no Youth, divine!
And lo the wretch! whose vile, whose insect lust
Lay'd this gay daughter of the Spring in dust.
Oh punish him, or to th'Elysian shades
Dismiss my soul, where no Carnation fades.
He ceas'd, and wept. With innocence of mien,
Th'Accus'd stood forth, and thus address'd the Queen.
Of all th'enamel'd race, whose silv'ry wing
Waves to the tepid Zephyrs of the spring,
Or swims along the fluid atmosphere,
Once brightest shin'd this child of Heat and Air.
I saw, and started from its vernal bow'r
The rising game, and chac'd from flow'r to flow'r.
It fled, I follow'd; now in hope, now pain;
It stopt, I stopt; it mov'd, I mov'd again.
At last it fix'd, 'twas on what plant it pleas'd,
And where it fix'd, the beauteous bird I seiz'd:
Rose or Carnation was below my care;
I meddle, Goddess! only in my sphere.
I tell the naked fact without disguise,
And, to excuse it, need but shew the prize;
Whose spoils this paper offers to your eye,
Fair ev'n in death! this peerless *Butterfly.*
My sons! (she answer'd) both have done your parts:
Live happy both, and long promote our arts.
But hear a Mother, when she recommends
To your fraternal care, our sleeping friends.
The common Soul, of Heav'n's more frugal make,
Serves but to keep fools pert, and knaves awake:
A drowzy Watchman, that just gives a knock,
And breaks our rest, to tell us what's a clock.
Yet by some object ev'ry brain is stirr'd;

The dull may waken to a Humming–bird;
The most recluse, discreetly open'd, find
Congenial matter in the Cockle–kind;
The mind, in Metaphysics at a loss,
May wander in a wilderness of Moss;
The head that turns at super–lunar things,
Poiz'd with a tail, may steer on Wilkins' wings.
O! would the Sons of Men once think their Eyes
And Reason giv'n them but to study *Flies*!

See Nature in some partial narrow shape,
And let the Author of the Whole escape:
Learn but to trifle; or, who most observe,
To wonder at their Maker, not to serve.
Be that my task (replies a gloomy Clerk,
Sworn foe to Myst'ry, yet divinely dark;
Whose pious hope aspires to see the day
When Moral Evidence shall quite decay,
And damns implicit faith, and holy lies,
Prompt to impose, and fond to dogmatize:)
Let others creep by timid steps, and slow,
On plain Experience lay foundations low,

By common sense to common knowledge bred,
And last, to Nature's Cause thro' Nature led.
All–seeing in thy mists, we want no guide,
Mother of Arrogance, and Source of Pride!
We nobly take the high Priori Road,
And reason downward, till we doubt of God:
Make Nature still incroach upon his plan;
And shove him off as far as e'er we can:
Thrust some Mechanic Cause into his place;
Or bind in Matter, or diffuse in Space.

Or, at one bound o'er–leaping all his laws,
Make God Man's Image, Man the final Cause,

Find Virtue local, all Relation scorn,
See all in *Self*, and but for self be born:
Of nought so certain as our *Reason* still,
Of nought so doubtful as of *Soul* and *Will.*
Oh hide the God still more! and make us see
Such as Lucretius drew, a God like Thee:

Wrapt up in Self, a God without a Thought,
Regardless of our merit or default.
Or that bright Image to our fancy draw,
Which Theocles in raptur'd vision saw,

While thro' Poetic scenes the Genius roves,
Or wanders wild in Academic Groves;
That Nature our Society adores,
Where Tindal dictates, and Silenus snores.
Rous'd at his name, up rose the bowzy Sire,
And shook from out his Pipe the seeds of fire;
Then snapt his box, and strok'd his belly down:
Rosy and rev'rend, tho' without a Gown.
Bland and familiar to the throne he came,
Led up the Youth, and call'd the Goddess *Dame*.
Then thus. From Priest–craft happily set free,
Lo! ev'ry finish'd Son returns to thee:

First slave to Words, then vassal to a Name,
Then dupe to Party; child and man the same;
Bounded by Nature, narrow'd still by Art,
A trifling head, and a contracted heart.
Thus bred, thus taught, how many have I seen,
Smiling on all, and smil'd on by a Queen.
Mark'd out for Honours, honour'd for their Birth,
To thee the most rebellious things on earth:
Now to thy gentle shadow all are shrunk,
All melted down, in Pension, or in Punk!
So K— so B— sneak'd into the grave,

A Monarch's half, and half a Harlot's slave.
Poor W— nipt in Folly's broadest bloom,
Who praises now? his Chaplain on his Tomb.
Then take them all, oh take them to thy breast!
Thy *Magus*, Goddess! shall perform the rest.
With that, a Wizard old his *Cup* extends;
Which whoso tastes, forgets his former friends,

Sire, Ancestors, Himself. One casts his eyes
Up to a *Star*, and like Endymion dies:
A *Feather* shooting from another's head,
Extracts his brain, and Principle is fled,
Lost is his God, his Country, ev'ry thing;
And nothing left but Homage to a King!

The vulgar herd turn off to roll with Hogs,
To run with Horses, or to hunt with Dogs;
But, sad example! never to escape
Their Infamy, still keep the human shape.
But she, good Goddess, sent to ev'ry child
Firm Impudence, or Stupefaction mild;
And strait succeeded, leaving shame no room,
Cibberian forehead, or Cimmerian gloom.
Kind Self–conceit to some her glass applies,
Which no one looks in with another's eyes:
But as the Flatt'rer or Dependant paint,
Beholds himself a Patriot, Chief, or Saint.
On others Int'rest her gay liv'ry flings,
Int'rest, that waves on Party–colour'd wings:
Turn'd to the Sun, she casts a thousand dyes,
And, as she turns, the colours fall or rise.
Others the Syren Sisters warble round,
And empty heads console with empty sound.
No more, alas! the voice of Fame they hear,
The balm of Dulness trickling in their ear.
Great C—, H—, P—, R—, K—,

Why all your Toils? your Sons have learn'd to sing.
How quick Ambition hastes to ridicule!
The Sire is made a Peer, the Son a Fool.
On some, a Priest succinct in amice white
Attends; all flesh is nothing in his sight!
Beeves, at his touch, at once to jelly turn,
And the huge Boar is shrunk into an Urn:
The board with specious miracles he loads,
Turns Hares to Larks, and Pigeons into Toads.

Another (for in all what one can shine?)
Explains the *Seve* and *Verdeur* of the Vine.
What cannot copious Sacrifice attone?
Thy Treufles, Perigord! thy Hams, Bayonne!
With French Libation, and Italian Strain,
Wash Bladen white, and expiate Hays's stain.
Knight lifts the head, for what are crowds undone
To three essential Partriges in one?
Gone ev'ry blush, and silent all reproach,
Contending Princes mount them in their Coach.
Next bidding all draw near on bended knees,
The Queen confers her *Titles* and *Degrees*.
Her children first of more distinguish'd sort,
Who study Shakespeare at the Inns of Court,
Impale a Glow–worm, or Vertù profess,
Shine in the dignity of F. R. S.
Some, deep Free–Masons, join the silent race
Worthy to fill Pythagoras's place:
Some Botanists, or Florists at the least,
Or issue Members of an Annual feast.
Nor past the meanest unregarded, one
Rose a Gregorian, one a Gormogon.
The last, not least in honour or applause,
Isis and Cam made Doctors of her Laws.
Then blessing all, Go Children of my care!
To Practice now from Theory repair.

All my commands are easy, short, and full:
My Sons! be proud, be selfish, and be dull.

Guard my Prerogative, assert my Throne:
This Nod confirms each Privilege your own.
The Cap and Switch be sacred to his Grace;
With Staff and Pumps the Marquis lead the Race;
From Stage to Stage the licens'd Earl may run,
Pair'd with his Fellow–Charioteer the Sun;
The learned Baron Butterflies design,
Or draw to silk Arachne's subtile line;
The Judge to dance his brother Sergeant call;
The Senator at Cricket urge the Ball;

The Bishop stow (Pontific Luxury!)
An hundred Souls of Turkeys in a pye;
The sturdy Squire to Gallic masters stoop,
And drown his Lands and Manors in a Soupe.
Others import yet nobler arts from France,
Teach Kings to fiddle, and make Senates dance.
Perhaps more high some daring son may soar,
Proud to my list to add one Monarch more;
And nobly conscious, Princes are but things
Born for First Ministers, as Slaves for Kings,
Tyrant supreme! shall three Estates command,
And make one Mighty Dunciad of the Land!
More she had spoke, but yawn'd—All Nature nods:
What Mortal can resist the Yawn of Gods?
Churches and Chapels instantly it reach'd;
(St. James's first, for leaden Gilbert preach'd)

Then catch'd the Schools; the Hall scarce kept awake;
The Convocation gap'd, but could not speak:
Lost was the Nation's Sense, nor could be found,
While the long solemn Unison went round:
Wide, and more wide, it spread o'er all the realm;

Ev'n Palinurus nodded at the Helm:
The Vapour mild o'er each Committee crept;
Unfinish'd Treaties in each Office slept;
And Chiefless Armies doz'd out the Campaign;
And Navies yawn'd for Orders on the Main.
O Muse! relate (for you can tell alone,
Wits have short Memories, and Dunces none)
Relate, who first, who last resign'd to rest;
Whose Heads she partly, whose completely blest;
What Charms could Faction, what Ambition lull,
The Venal quiet, and intrance the Dull;
'Till drown'd was Sense, and Shame, and Right, and Wrong—
O sing, and hush the Nations with thy Song!
In vain, in vain,—the all–composing Hour
Resistless falls: The Muse obeys the Pow'r.

She comes! she comes! the sable Throne behold
Of *Night* Primæval, and of *Chaos* old!
Before her, *Fancy*'s gilded clouds decay,
And all its varying Rain–bows die away.
Wit shoots in vain its momentary fires,
The meteor drops, and in a flash expires.
As one by one, at dread Medea's strain,
The sick'ning stars fade off th'ethereal plain;
As Argus' eyes by Hermes' wand opprest,
Clos'd one by one to everlasting rest;
Thus at her felt approach, and secret might,
Art after *Art* goes out, and all is Night.
See skulking *Truth* to her old Cavern fled,
Mountains of Casuistry heap'd o'er her head!
Philosophy, that lean'd on Heav'n before,
Shrinks to her second cause, and is no more.

Physic of *Metaphysic* begs defence,
And *Metaphysic* calls for aid on *Sense*!
See *Mystery* to *Mathematics* fly!

In vain! they gaze, turn giddy, rave, and die.

Religion blushing veils her sacred fires,
And unawares *Morality* expires.
Nor *public* Flame, nor *private*, dares to shine;
Nor *human* Spark is left, nor Glimpse *divine*!
Lo! thy dread Empire, Chaos! is restor'd;
Light dies before thy uncreating word:
Thy hand, great Anarch! lets the curtain fall;
And Universal Darkness buries All.

FINIS.

Printed in the United States
65194LVS00004B/17